Brown Boy Brown Boy What Can You Be?

Written By:

Ameshia Gabriel Arthur

DEDICATION

To Matthew and Benjamin. You are each my heart beat on two feet. To all of my brown boys, you are essential to our survival. You are important and we need you. I love you.

Brown boy, brown boy, what can you be?

I can be the winner of a spelling bee.

I can be a graduate with a college degree.

I can be a ship captain exploring the sea.

I can be an artist on a creative spree.

I can be a pilot flying high and free.

I can be a horticulturist who takes care of the flowers and trees.

Brown boy, brown boy, what can you be?

I can be a scientist who studies bumblebees.

I can be a great orator with my name on a marquee.

I can be a meteorologist whom predicts the weather and degree.

I can be an oceanographer focusing on algae.

I can be an inventor who makes life easy.

I can be a chef known for my delicious curry.

I can be a role model for brown boys like me.

I am a valuable part of my community.

ABOUT THE AUTHOR

I am Ameshia. I am a brown girl. I am a lover of brown boys, brown girls, and beautiful people. I believe in kindness and representation. I believe literacy, information, and understanding are foundations of freedom. Love and be free.

Made in the USA
Lexington, KY
25 May 2019